Excerpted from

Benjamin Graham

The Memoirs of the
Dean of Wall Street

McGraw-Hill

New York   San Francisco   Washington, D.C.   Auckland   Bogotá
Caracas   Lisbon   London   Madrid   Mexico City   Milan
Montreal   New Delhi   San Juan   Singapore
Sydney   Tokyo   Toronto

McGraw-Hill

A Division of The McGraw·Hill Companies

1 2 3 4 5 6 7 8 9 0 9 0 9 0 1 0 9 8 7 6

ISBN 0-07-135509-X

All photographs courtesy of the Graham family collection.

This book is printed on acid-free paper.

Introduction to This Excerpt

When Benjamin Graham died in 1976 at age 82, he had achieved legendary status on Wall Street. He had laid the foundation of modern security analysis, inspiring legions of disciples and personally mentoring such up-and-comers as Warren Buffett (who went to work for Graham in 1954). Graham was widely regarded as brilliant, successful, and ethical—a rare trinity of attributes in the rough-and-tumble world of investing.

It is unusual that we have access into a mind so powerful and so influential. Yet Benjamin Graham himself has provided us with the opportunity to know the man behind the theories. In his sixties and seventies, Graham retired and wrote an account of his life. He put down as much as he could remember of his family and business life, and of the sights and sounds of his hometown of New York City. Renowned for his capacious memory, Graham sought to write not just a record of his life, but an honest assessment.

Upon a complete reading of *Benjamin Graham: The Memoirs of the Dean of Wall Street*, it is clear that this memoir is a personal account, not a practical guide to investment. Still, the insights into Graham's early life that emerge within the book's pages suggest how he got to be the superb investor that he was.

This excerpt includes:

- A chronology of the most important events that shaped Benjamin Graham throughout his life
- *Chapter Nine, The Beginnings of Real Success*, which chronicles Graham's spectacular progress on Wall Street between 1919 and 1929

- *Chapter Ten, The Great Bull Market of the 1920s: I Become a Near Millionaire,* in which Graham recounts the opening of his own firm and some of the ethical questions he pondered about the brokerage industry
- *Chapter Sixteen, The Commodity Reserve Currency Plan,* which entails Graham's development of the underlying theory to most of his subsequent economic theories, including value investing

Chronology

On Dean Keppel's advice decides to follow a career in finance. Refuses three possible teaching jobs at Columbia. Tutors General Leonard Wood's son. Teaches English to foreign students at Bronx night school. Moves to luxurious Hunt's Point Palace apartments. Is invited by Carl Van Doren to be instructor at Brierly School but refuses. Hears Yvette Guilbert reciting a war poem. Because of anti-German sentiment, family changes name from Grossbaum to Graham. Joins brokerage firm of Newburger, Henderson, and Loeb. Writes evaluation of Missouri Pacific Railroad that prompts an offer from J.S. Bache and Company as security analyst, but Newburger refuses to let him go.

1915 Meets Hazel Mazur. Gives up night school job, but continues teaching officers' sons on Governors Island. Works as board-boy in customers' room at Newburger. Speculates in Missouri Pacific stock and is censured by Newburger. Completes successful arbitrage analysis of Guggenheim Exploration Company. Buys first auto jointly with Cousin Lou. Donates his sets of Hebbel and Lessing to Columbia University Library.

1916 Announces engagement to Hazel. Salary is raised to $50 per week. U.S. Express in bankruptcy. Negotiates purchase of house securities for Newburger Company; also acts as the company's bookmaker for bets on the presidential election.

1917 Marries Hazel. Brother Leon also marries. Opens unsuccessful phonograph shop venture with brothers, selling at a loss in 1919. Draft board grants deferment. Joins army reserve. Invests money for Professor Tassin, and loses it in mini-crash, then repays Tassin at $60 per month. Publishes article in *The American Mathematical Monthly*.

1918 Mother moves in; tension between her and Hazel. Makes brief effort as business consultant with Maurice Gerard, his mother's elder brother. First child, Isaac

Newton, born. Writes article for *The Magazine of Wall Street* explaining how to determine value of goodwill; will write dozens more for this magazine over the years.

1919 Finishes army reserve training. Does comparative analysis of railroad bonds. Rises in Wall Street. The bull market of 1919. Makes killing on Savold Tire, then loses money to syndicate organizer's trickery. After negative analysis of Chicago, Milwaukee, & St. Paul, meets Robert J. Marony, its vice-president, who becomes lifelong friend and later associate. Manages successful call operation with Pierce Oil bonds.

1920 Becomes junior partner in Newburger, Henderson, and Loeb. Conducts highly successful dealings in Japanese bonds with his friend Junkichi Miki. Starts a circular newsletter with assistance of Leo Stern. Analyzes tire industry. Accepts $20,000 investment from Uncle Maurice Gerard, who wishes to retire and live off the income. Becomes naturalized American citizen. Moves to Mt. Vernon. First daughter, Marjorie, born.

1921 Recommends trade of short-term U.S. Victory bonds for longer-term U.S. bonds and is proven correct. Idea for commodity reserve currency plan fermenting.

1922 Maurice Gerard and family move back to New York to be near Graham and Wall Street.

1923 Leaves Newburger and sets up private investment account, the Graham Corporation, with Harris family. Executes successful Du Pont–General Motors arbitrage. Buys stock in U.S. Express, now in liquidation.

1924 Takes a ski vacation in Mahopac with Hazel and two children, Newton and Marjorie.

1925 Graham Corporation dissolves as the Harrises drop out. Also dissolves Graham-Cohen account (with Benjamin V. Cohen). Second daughter, Elaine, is born. Spends summer in Deal, New Jersey.

1926 Sets up new structure, the "Benjamin Graham Joint

Account," in which he gets percentage of profit only. Investors put in $400,000. Jerome Newman joins firm, then becomes partner. Discovers undervaluation of Northern Pipeline. Summers again in Deal.

1927 At stockholders' meeting, requests that Northern Pipeline pay out surpluses to stockholders but loses because of lack of a second. Meets John D. Rockefeller. Son Newton dies of meningitis. Begins to teach at Columbia. Meets Bernard Baruch. Meets Winston Churchill. David Dodd becomes his student, then colleague. Hazel goes to Europe.

1928 Wins proxy fight with Northern Pipeline, becoming a director, as the company agrees to distribute excess holdings to stockholders. Becomes codirector of the ill-fated Unexcelled Fireworks Company. Newton II is born. Visits Europe. Moves to an expensive duplex in Beresford Apartments. Starts teaching enormously popular Advanced Security Analysis at Columbia (and continues till 1954).

1929 Joint account worth 2½ million; Bernard Baruch offers him partnership, which he refuses. Vacations on Baruch's brother's yacht. Agrees with Baruch that Crash is imminent, but unlike Baruch, leaves portion of portfolio in stock market. Account shows 20 percent loss for year.

1930 Joint account's worst financial year, down 50 percent. Receives no income from the joint account for five years. Lives by teaching, writing, and consulting. Marriage to Hazel is becoming shaky.

1931 Joint account down 16 percent.

1932 Joint account down 3 percent (70 percent of the original 2½ million has been lost). Chairs protective committee to secure proceeds of preferred stock in Aeolian record company. Moves to less luxurious apartment, the El Dorado. Dow Jones average is 42. Makes presentation to Economic Forum at the New School for Social

Research on Commodity Reserve Currency Plan. Publishes three-part series called "Is American Business Worth More Dead Than Alive?" in *Forbes*.

1933 Account is worth $375,000. Makes 50 percent profit. Publishes article in *Economic Forum*. Writes plays *China Wedding* and *The Day of Reckoning*, but they are not produced. Appears in court for first time as expert witness; will do forty more over the years.

1934 First Edition of *Security Analysis* published by McGraw-Hill (later editions appear in 1940, 1951, 1962, and 1988). Third daughter, Winifred, is born. Fund proposes to pay Graham and Newman straight 20 percent of profits. His play *Baby Pompadour* (earlier called *True to the Marines*) appears on Broadway on December 27 at the Vanderbilt Theatre and closes after four performances. The Fund adopts new financial accounting methods. Is consulted by government about the proposed Securities Exchange Act.

1935 All Depression losses have now been made good. Helps found New York Society of Security Analysts.

1936 Under IRS pressure, changes the joint account to "The Graham-Newman Corporation." Meets Carol Wade on cruise.

1937 Publishes *Storage and Stability* (McGraw-Hill) and *The Interpretation of Financial Statements* with Charles McGolrick (Harper and Row, Second Edition, 1955). Carol becomes his mistress. He proposes divorce to Hazel. When she refuses he goes to Reno over his lawyer's protest. Hazel finally agrees, and she obtains a divorce in Reno.

1938 Marries Carol at Sherry Netherlands Hotel in New York City.

1940 Divorces Carol. Revised Edition of *Security Analysis*. A lonely bachelor, he takes up roller-skating and attending Brooklyn Dodgers' baseball games. Starts a relationship with his secretary Estelle Messing, whom he later marries.

1941   Addresses American Statistical Association in Hartford on "A Program for Stabilizing the Purchasing Power of the Dollar."

1942   Proposes a board of qualifiers for the New York Society of Security Analysts.

1943   Has final contact with Carol Wade. First grandchild, Cathy Janis, is born to Marjorie (will have ten more grandchildren).

1944   Mother is murdered in robbery on walk home from her bridge game. Marries Estelle Messing. Publishes *World Commodities and World Currency* (McGraw-Hill).

1945   Meets John D. Rockefeller for third time at New York State Chamber of Commerce banquet. Defends Full Employment Act to this unreceptive audience. Benjamin Jr. is born. Begins to write articles for *The Analysts Journal* (later called *The Financial Analysts Journal*), first under the pseudonym "Cogitator" and later under his own name.

1946   Addresses Summer Institute for Social Progress, Wellesley, Massachusetts on "Our Economic Future, Its Direction and Control." Engages in a public debate with Floyd Odlum (chairman of the Atlas Corporation, friend of Howard Hughes, and husband of Jacqueline Cochran) about the wisdom of buying distressed companies.

1947   Meets Dwight D. Eisenhower. Speaks at the first annual conference of the Financial Analysts Federation (later the Institute of Chartered Financial Analysts), urging formal certification examinations and standards for the profession.

1948   Buys controlling interest in GEICO, then takes it public.

1949   Writes and publishes *The Intelligent Investor* (Second Edition, 1954; Third, 1959; Fourth, 1973, the last with help from Warren Buffett). Forms the Graham-Newman Partnership.

1950   Becomes member of board of P & R Company, owner of coal and railroad properties.

1951 Serves as president of the Jewish Guild for the Blind (until 1953). Moves course to the Columbia Graduate School of Business.

1952 Addresses Institute of Chartered Financial Analysts on "Toward a Science of Security Analysis."

1953 Writes "Stock Dividends" for *Barron's*.

1954 Hires Warren Buffett. Graham-Newman now capitalized at $6 million. Travels to France to retrieve belongings of Newton II, a Korean War veteran, who has committed suicide. Begins a correspondence with Malou, with whom he falls in love. Over the years they spend more and more time together.

1955 Explains his success in testimony before a Senate committee chaired by James Fulbright. Elaine receives Ph.D. in Psychology at Yale University.

1956 Dissolves Graham-Newman Corporation and Graham-Newman Partnership and retires to Beverly Hills with Estelle and Benjamin Jr. Lives at 611 North Maple across the street from his cousin Rhoda Gerard Sarnat and her husband Dr. Bernard Sarnat. Becomes Regents Professor at the Graduate School of Business of UCLA, where he teaches without pay for fifteen years.

1957 Writes autobiographical vignettes.

1958 Testifies before House Ways and Means Committee on dividend policy, margin rules, and capital gains taxes (which he favors preserving).

1959 Gives up tennis.

1960 Visits London home.

1962 His effort to professionalize security analysts leads to the creation of the Financial Analysts Federation, later named the Association for Investment Management and Research, which gives certification by examination to financial analysts. Publishes Fourth Edition of *Security Analysis* with Sidney Cottle and Charles Tatham. (A Fifth Edition published in 1988 under auspices of Frank Block.)

1963   Sits for a portrait by the Dutch painter Jan Hoowig, paid for by Buffett and other ex-students and donated to the Financial Analysts Federation.

1964   Marjorie publishes *A Two-Year-Old Goes to Nursery School: A Case Study of Separation Reactions* (Tavistock Press). His friend's son Andrew Goodman, like Benjamin Jr., a volunteer in the Southern Voting Rights movement, is killed in Mississippi.

1965   Resigns from GEICO Board of Directors.

1966   Moves to La Jolla (7811 Eads Avenue) with Malou. They continue to live there for part of the year and divide the rest of their time between Malou's home in Aix-en-Provence and (for a time) Funchal, Madeira.

1967   Publishes his translation of a Uruguayan novel, Mario Benedetti's *The Truce*, with Harper and Row.

1968   Warren Buffett and other old students of Graham make a pilgrimage to seek his advice about the market. They meet at the Hotel Del Coronado. Corresponds with "Adam Smith," author of *The Money Game*.

1970   Takes trip to Australia.

1971   Jerry Newman resigns from GEICO Board of Directors.

1974   Eightieth birthday celebration: delivers speech and is presented by his brother Victor with a printed volume of his poems. Gives lecture on the "Renaissance of Value" to Institute of Chartered Financial Analysts, urging analysts to buy stocks at "fire-sale" prices (Dow is at 600) (excerpts printed in *Barron's*, September 23, 1974).

1975   Receives the Molodovsky Award, the highest given by the Financial Analysts Federation.

1976   With James Buchanan Rea cofounds the Rea-Graham Fund. Dies September 21, in Aix-en-Provence, France. Malou, Marjorie, and Elaine arrange for his cremation, and Marjorie carries his ashes back to the United States. The family holds a memorial and buries his ashes at Stephen Wise Free Synagogue Westchester Hills Cemetery at Hastings-on-Hudson, New York. A memorial service is held at Faculty House, Columbia University. Benjamin Jr. receives M.D. from University of California Medical School. GEICO on verge of bankruptcy, Buffett buys heavily into it, owning 48 percent by 1990 (and buying balance in 1995).

1977   First wife Hazel dies.

1979   Daughter Winifred Graham Downsbrough dies.

1981   Third wife Estelle Messing Graham dies.

1982   Rea-Graham becomes a public mutual fund.

1984   McGraw-Hill gives fiftieth anniversary celebration for *Security Analysis* at Columbia. Dodd is awarded honorary doctorate.

1986   Warren Buffett gives his famous speech, "The Superinvestors of Graham and Doddsville" (later published in *Hermes*, and in the last edition of *The Intelligent Investor*).

1987   David Dodd dies.

1988   Elected to the U.S. Business Hall of Fame in Atlanta. Other laureates include: Stephen Bechtel, Andrew Carnegie, Walter Chrysler, Walt Disney, Pierre Du Pont, George Eastman, Thomas Edison, Henry Ford, A. P. Giannini, Conrad Hilton, Henry Kaiser, Henry Luce, Andrew Mellon, J. Pierpont Morgan, Adolph Ochs, William Paley, J. C. Penney, John D. Rockefeller, David Sarnoff, Alfred Sloan, not to speak of Benjamin Franklin and George Washington. The award is accepted for the Graham family by Benjamin Jr. Robert Heilbrunn establishes a Professorship of Asset Management and Finance at Columbia Business School as the "cornerstone of a Graham and Dodd Research Institute."

CHAPTER NINE

The Beginnings of Real Success

Between 1919 and 1929 my upward progress in Wall Street was rapid, even spectacular. It was an exhilarating period, marked by many financial triumphs, a continuous advance in my standard of living, a widening and deepening of my knowledge of life's material and intellectual enjoyments, and a feeling of great satisfaction about my position in the world and the esteem of my fellow men. But there were developments also on the debit side. The loss of my first-born son in 1927 was a bitter blow, the more staggering perhaps because it came so suddenly in the midst of dazzling prosperity. There were also strains developing in my marriage, which neither Hazel nor I—as brilliant as we considered ourselves—had enough insight to recognize and act upon in time. I was too ready to accept materialistic success as the aim and goal of life and to forget about idealistic achievements.

At the beginning of 1920, I was made a junior partner in the firm of Newburger, Henderson, and Loeb, members of the New York Stock Exchange, a fact which was duly announced in newspaper advertisements. The new arrangement gave me—in addition to my salary—an interest of 2½ percent in the annual profits, without liability for any losses. The same promotion was conferred on Dan Loeb and Harold Rouse, who were my seniors in employment by two years. Mr. A. N. informed me that my divvy was a half-percent higher than Loeb's and Rouse's but added that I was not to divulge this fact to them. My share in the profits ran about $5,000 per annum during the four years that I enjoyed it.

That year I had my Japanese bond experience, a venture which assigned me a rather special position in Wall Street. One of my young friends, Lou Berall, had given up schoolteaching for a financial career and was working for Bonright & Company, an important bond house. We went to lunch from time to time, and on one occasion he brought along an exceedingly young Japanese named Junkichi Miki. This lively fellow had come to America as a representative of a large Japanese banking firm which had thought of selling American bond issues in Japan. Bonright & Company had undertaken to train him in American investment methods, hoping thus to find an outlet in Japan for some of their merchandise.

But things developed in an entirely different direction. Miki or his superiors soon discovered that large profits could be made by buying up various issues of Japanese government bonds which had been placed in various countries abroad during the Russo-Japanese War of 1906 and reselling them to investors in Japan. Their attractiveness to Japanese buyers grew out of postwar discrepancies in foreign exchange rates, on the one hand, and the right of investors to demand payment of principal and interest in fixed amounts of yen, on the other. The Japanese asked Bonright to cooperate with them in acquiring and importing these bonds in quantities into Japan, but the American firm was too busy with its own underwriting operations to take much interest.

At my luncheon with Berall and Miki, the young Japanese asked me whether our firm had European connections and other facilities to do this reacquisition business on a large scale. Fortunately, I could say we had and could offer him comprehensive and energetic service. After we had carried out one or two trial orders to his satisfaction, Miki was ready to make the big deal. He agreed to use our services exclusively for large-scale purchases, and we agreed to buy for no one but his firm, the Fujimoto Bill Broker Bank of Osaka. Bonds were to be shipped to Japan, draft attached. We were to receive a commission of 2 percent of each purchase, out of which we paid all expenses, including cable and shipping charges.

The business ran into the millions. We established good contacts with brokerage firms in London, Paris, and Amsterdam, which had been centers for the original distribution of the bonds. Because of the discounts of the franc against the yen, the bonds sold in Paris at enormous premiums over their par value and at the same time could be bought by the Japanese investor at a large discount, even after allowing for big brokerage expenses.

One aspect of this business made me rather unpopular in our back office. For some reason (which I have forgotten), a large portion of these bonds were first sold in America in $100 denominations, instead of the customary $1,000 or less frequent $500 pieces. The same had been true of the issues placed in Paris and London. These small pieces were considered a nuisance and sold at a substantial discount in the Western markets, but there was no prejudice against them in Japan. Miki was glad to buy them up at the cheaper price. As a result our office was constantly inundated with reams and reams of these bulky documents of small unit value. Our typical single purchase would be for $100,000 face amount, which would usually entail 1,000 separate bonds, each of which had not only to be counted but also inspected for possibly missing interest coupons.

Since we usually had a quantity of these bonds on hand waiting to be made up into a large shipment, we acquired a special safe deposit box for them. To our runners, who had to carry this heavy box to and from safe deposit vaults each day,

it was known, not too favorably, as the Ben Graham box. However, the business made millions and proved extremely profitable to the firm; our commissions must certainly have
exceeded $100,000. After about two years Miki set up his own
office, acquiring the bonds directly himself—a move which we
had regarded as inevitable and did not resent. In the mean-
time we had become extremely well known in Japanese financial circles. Two of their stock exchanges sent a delegation to
study our brokerage methods and techniques, with the view to
imitating them in Tokyo and Osaka. Miki brought them in to
see me; they picked my brains for a long time and departed
with a complete set of our numerous printed forms. Not long
thereafter they published a long report in Japanese on the
New York stock market, a copy of which was sent to me. I was
both startled and gratified to observe that after every few
pages there was inserted a reproduction of one of our forms
each bearing the name Newburger, Henderson, and Loeb in
our conspicuous type.

As we wound up business with the Fujimoto Bank, we
relaxed the exclusive clause of the arrangement, and each side
did business with other houses. We bought bonds on cabled
instruction from two other Japanese banking firms. These
cables used a five-letter code, which economized greatly on toll
charges. Despite many possibilities of ambiguity and error in
code messages, especially when one of the parties thinks in
Japanese, this business ran with remarkable smoothness for a
two-year period. We did, however, have one untoward incident
which illustrates the special efforts made by the Japanese to
build confidence in their business honesty and reliability. (Ori-
ental nations were then suspected of being crafty and double-
dealing.)

On a large order from a Tokyo banking firm, we bought several hundred thousand bonds, which we duly reported. But
they sent us a cable that read "Cancel order. Confirm." We
canceled the balance of the order, cabled back "Order canceled," and proceeded to ship the bonds they had bought.

When the bonds arrived in Tokyo a month later—there was no airmail in those days—our Tokyo friends were most unpleasantly surprised. They insisted that this purchase had been canceled and they were not responsible for it. We, of course, claimed that in Wall Street a "cancel order" refers only to an unexecuted order, and they should have cabled us "cancel purchase" (though it was too late to do that). It was stupid of me not to have made the point clearly in my cable.

The market had had a sinking spell during the shipment period, and a loss of several thousands had accrued. We took the matter up with the Yokohama Specie Bank in New York, which was a Japanese government agency and the official representative of their financial community. After a relatively short delay, they paid us in full for the bonds—although they could very well have suggested that, under the somewhat ambiguous circumstances, both parties divide the loss.

Miki and I became good friends. From time to time he came to our house and seemed to enjoy our Jewish cooking. In return he took me to a sumptuous dinner at the Nippon Club near Columbia University, where I had my first taste of Japanese food. To my own amazement, I found myself swallowing varieties of raw fish dipped in numerous sauces. But sitting on the floor for two hours proved an uncomfortable experience.

Miki introduced me to various Japanese VIPs from time to time, most of them figures in the financial world. One day he asked me if he could bring his friend, Mr. Kwagai, to lunch. Mr. Kwagai proved to be a handsome, stocky, amiable young man. During the meal we talked about Wall Street and miscellaneous matters. When we were leaving, Miki said with his invariable smile, "Mr. Graham, perhaps you would like to see Mr. Kwagai play at Forest Hills some day next week. If so, I shall be glad to get you a ticket." Only then did I realize that I had been lunching with the famous Japanese tennis player who had a good chance to win the American singles championship. And we hadn't spoken a word about tennis, my favorite sport! How dumb or unlucky can a fellow be?

Thirty-five years later I visited Japan and renewed my friendship with Junkichi Miki. After his return to Japan, he had become an official of the Osaka Stock Exchange, and then a professor of finance at Kobe University. He took me to visit the Osaka Exchange and its officials. I was ushered into their directors' room where a large group were seated. The introductions completed, Miki said blandly to me, "And now, Mr. Graham, will you kindly give this assemblage a forty-minute talk on the principles of security analysis? I shall be glad to translate what you say." This was certainly more than I had bargained for, but I did the best I could under the circumstances. At the end of each sentence or two, Professor Miki unhesitatingly translated my highly technical language into Japanese, and there would be a nodding of comprehending heads around the room.

During this renewal of friendship with Miki, I was taken to the best Osaka restaurants and introduced to that wonderful institution, the Geisha girl. In consideration of its numerous American guests, one of the restaurants had a sort of well dug under the low table. In this way one could sit on the floor with one's legs hanging down, a much more comfortable arrangement for Westerners than the other. The Geishas were beautiful, gorgeously dressed, highly accomplished in song and dance and on the tamisen and continuously attentive to their patrons during the long meal. They had a rather limited knowledge of American dances, but mine graciously allowed me to teach her an additional step or two. We played a few harmless games and altogether had a delightful time. Will it ever be possible for us to introduce this completely moral institution into America for the delectation of the tired or not-so-tired businessman and bon vivant by persuading oversuspicious wives that such an amenity would actually contribute to happiness in marriage?

Back to 1920: Miki came to our house one evening asking to be taught how to play poker. I instructed him according to Hoyle, and he carefully wrote down the values of the various hands in a little notebook. After some rounds of play, during which he sedulously compared his hands with his notebook, he declared himself satisfied and ready to play with his friends. A few days later I asked him how he had made out. "Ah, Mr. Graham," shaking his head sadly, "You were a very imperfect instructor. I lost a lot of money to my friends." "My goodness," I replied, "what did I tell you that was wrong?" "You didn't tell me anything wrong. You just forgot to tell me about bluff. They bluffed me all night long, and when the game was over, they never stopped teasing me about it." I felt so ashamed of my inexcusable omission that I even offered to make up his losses, but he refused with true Japanese dignity.

I was in complete charge of the "statistical" department at N.H.&L., which now bears the more respectable title of "research" or "investment research." My assistant was a former college mate, Leo Stern, about two years my junior. When I left, Leo took over most of my functions; in due course he became junior partner, full partner, and finally one of two senior partners—the other being Lester Newburger, the youngest of the four brothers I had worked under. Leo and I handled all inquiries, whether in person or by mail, about security lists or individual issues. From time to time we issued circulars which analyzed one or more securities in considerable detail. These generally included recommendations to buy a favored issue or to switch from a less to a more attractive security. For example, we recommended in 1921 that holders of U.S. Victory 4¾s, due in two years and selling at 97¾, should exchange them for the longer-term U.S. 4¼s which could be had for a lower price, around 87½. It was our view—correct, as it turned out—that the then high interest rates would subside and that the long-term governments would advance to par or better, while the short-term ones had very limited possibilities of gain. Our circular was advertised in the newspapers under the title "Memorandum to Holders of Victory Bonds." Promptly after it appeared, the New York Stock Exchange asked to see a copy. There had been an unwritten but stringent rule prohibiting stock exchange members from recommending switches out of government bonds into other securities. But they had no criticism to make of our proposal, which was not only unobjectionable from the patriotic angle but proved quite profitable to those who adopted it.

Another circular, not so smart, was of a routine variety, carrying a detailed comparison of all the listed tire and rubber stocks. On the basis of the statistical record, we observed that the shares of Ajax Tire appeared most attractive. A few days later a tall, handsome gentleman strode into our office, identified himself as Horace de Lisser, president of Ajax Tire, and demanded to see the author of the circular. He was the more noticeable figure because he was wearing a straw hat in the midst of winter—one of his several idiosyncrasies. As my cousin Miriam, then my secretary, delights to tell the story, Horace de Lisser was directed towards our department, found me doing something just outside my office, and in an imperious voice commanded: "Boy, take me in to see Mr. Graham." His error in taking me for an office boy may have been due in good part to myopia but also to the fact that I was young for my advanced position and looked quite a bit younger. (This impression persisted for years and gave rise to a variety of incidents.) I don't know which of us was the more nonplussed—he to see a young kid analyzing his industry, or I to be confronted by the strange man with a straw hat. The interview was rather strained. A number of years later I came to regret that circular and to wish I had visited Mr. de Lisser before I had published it. Ajax Tire flourished only a little while and then declined into bankruptcy.

One of the most important and rewarding friendships of my life grew out of one of my analytical circulars and in quite unexpected fashion. In 1919, I was working on a detailed comparison of two railroads—the Chicago, Milwaukee, & St. Paul Railroad and the St. Louis & Southwestern Railroad. Let me digress for a moment about nomenclature. Railroads were referred to in our business by special names. When I was just starting at the firm, I heard Murphy, our senior order clerk, refer to something as "shortstop." I thought he was saying "short stock," and I kept wondering how anyone could buy a hundred shares of "short stock," but I didn't dare to ask Murph for an explanation. He was actually referring to St. Louis & Southwestern Railroad, whose ticker-tape abbreviation was "SS." As for the Chicago, Milwaukee, & St. Paul, the railway was generally known as the "Milwaukee," but not on the stock exchange, where the nickname was based on the ticker abbreviations. The most amusing example was the Atchison, Topeka, & Santa Fe. No railroadman or customer would ever dream of calling it anything but the Santa Fe. But for countless years its ticker symbol was ATCH, and so it was always called "Atchison" or "Atch" in Wall Street. For some mysterious reason, the Dutch stock exchange dubbed it "Topeka." So this mighty railroad was known in three different markets by each of the three cities in its title.

Before I entered Wall Street, there had been both a preferred and common stock of the Northern Pacific Railroad, and they had been known to all the financial world, respectively, as "Big Nipper" and "Little Nipper." The preferred had been retired, as an aftermath of the famous Northern Pacific corner and panic of 1901, but thirteen years later I often heard people referring to the common stock as "Little Nipper." A much more harmful instance of this penchant for special nomenclature concerned the Great Northern Railway, the neighbor, rival, and one-time partner of Northern Pacific. As a result of its financial maneuvers, its own common stock had been retired, and its original preferred took the place of the common, being in every way equivalent to any other common stock. Yet for countless years it bore both the official and unofficial title of "Great Northern Preferred"; it was listed by Wall Street houses among the railroad preferred issues for investment; and it was naturally thought by most Wall Street amateurs to have the special protection of a preferred stock. It took some years before this inexcusable misbranding was corrected by the New York Stock Exchange.

Then there was the metamorphosis of the term "Big Steel." When U.S. Steel started its fluctuating career on the stock exchange in 1901, the higher-priced preferred was immediately dubbed "Big Steel," and the extremely speculative junior issue became known as "Little Steel"—as in the case of Big and Little Nipper. Eventually the price of Steel common passed that of the preferred, something that few Wall Streeters of 1901 would have predicted, and the old nicknames fell into disfavor. One day I was startled to hear an analyst use the term "Big Steel," but to find out that he was referring to U.S. Steel *common*. It had become "Big Steel" because its company was the largest. No doubt a long essay could be written about the vicissitudes of Wall Street nicknames.

To get back to the story: my comparative analysis of the Milwaukee and SS showed quite convincingly that SS common and preferred were more attractive buys than the correspondingly priced issues of the Milwaukee. Indeed, the Milwaukee appeared in a highly unfavorable light, so I felt it would be both fair and prudent to submit my findings to an officer of the company before publishing the circular. I went to see the financial vice-president of Milwaukee, Mr. Robert J. Marony, who had his office at 42 Broadway. He was surprisingly young for a railroad vice-president, only about forty or so, a little Irishman with a lively intelligent glance. With some embarrassment I told him why I had come. He looked over my material rather rapidly, then handed it back to me, saying: "I don't find anything to quarrel with in either your facts or your conclusions. I wish our showing was a better one, but it isn't, and that's that." Then he asked me some questions about my work in general. Soon we were talking about arbitrage, which was becoming one of my specialties, and in which he too was quite knowledgeable. I mentioned an interesting situation which was new to him. He listened intently to my explanation and then gave me an order to do a thousand shares for him. This was the least likely outcome that could have been predicted for my visit to the Chicago, Milwaukee, & St. Paul office.

That strange episode was the beginning of a business and personal association which has lasted until the present day (June 1960). Bob Marony became an investor in the Benjamin Graham Joint Account, then a substantial stockholder and director of Graham-Newman Corporation from its inception to its dissolution, a member of various protective committees which we organized, and finally a director with me of the fabulously successful Government Employee Insurance Group (GEICO). We have been good friends through prosperous and tough times. Once he gave me part of a profit on a successful deal because he thought I needed the money to help me out of personal financial difficulties. Some years before that he, his wife, Beatrice, and his daughter Marjorie, were my guests on Dr. Herman Baruch's yacht, the *Reposo*, which the amiable physician-turned-stockholder had lent me. Not so long after that happy trip, Bob and Bea were to lose their only child under especially tragic circumstances. The perennially youthful Marony suffered a stroke some years ago while in our office, and he has never recovered full control over his speech.

In these thirty-eight years of close association, Bob and I have never had a disagreement over anything. This is a remarkable record, considering the financial vicissitudes we went through together, the numerous important matters on which difficult decisions had to be made, the necessity for reaching agreement on such ticklish matters as division of profits and other forms of compensation, and, finally, the not unnatural tendency of Marony to get his Irish up from time to time—but always against someone other than me. Yet I must confess, in honesty and with regret, that even Bob, whom I have liked as much as any man on earth, was never a pal or crony. Perhaps I can sum it up in a single phrase: we never hung out together. What a simple, easy thing that seems to be for some people—and how elusive I have always found it!

I made a literary effort on behalf of N.H.&L., a series of three little pamphlets, bearing the title "Lessons for Investors." At the cocky age of twenty-five, I didn't realize the pretentiousness of that title nor my arrogance in presuming to instruct an investment public that averaged at least twice my age. Yet I believe that what I said made good sense. I am particularly proud of my strong argument for the purchase of sound common stocks at reasonable prices. Its crux was the then revolutionary statement that "if a common stock is a good investment, it is also an attractive speculation." For, said I, if it gives the investor full value for his money, if its market value is substantially less than its intrinsic value, it should also have excellent prospects for an advance in price. This was indeed a sound conclusion so long as the huge general public didn't act upon it. When that happened, several years later in the great bull market of the 1920s, investors forgot all about the safeguard of a responsible price and thus turned what formerly were sound investments into the most exaggerated and dangerous speculations.

My work as security analyst was by no means the major part of my job as junior partner. In addition, I handled all the operations of the firm for its own account (these being limited to arbitrage and hedging); I was the tax expert; I did the over-the-counter trading (including the Japanese bond operation); I was in charge of insuring the efficiency of the office systems; and, of course, I had a growing number of customers of various kinds who paid substantial commissions to the firm.

After World War I, U.S. tax laws and regulations—blessedly simple before—became increasingly complicated as well as onerous. I studied the subject quite thoroughly because of its bearing on the earnings of the corporations I was analyzing. The fact that I knew a little more than other people soon made me an expert, and I earned modest fees by making out tax returns for several of our customers. Towards the end of 1920 many of these suffered substantial paper losses on securities, while at the same time finding themselves subject to large taxes on their regular income. Like human beings everywhere, they were reluctant to sell those securities, believing that they would come back. I pointed out, citing chapter and verse from the income tax law, that such stocks could be sold, to establish the loss, and immediately bought back to reinstate the position. The cost of the operation would be limited to commissions and transfer tax. When the word got out, we received a large number of these lucrative "sell and buy" orders. I flatter myself that we were the first firm to execute such orders on the New York Stock Exchange, but before the end of the year everyone was doing it. (The next year, I think, Congress ended that picnic by requiring a thirty-day interval between sale and repurchase.)

My most ambitious research into the tax law and its consequences had to do with a calculation of the then jealously guarded goodwill or "water" component in corporate balance sheets. The excess-profits tax of 1917 allowed a credit of certain percentages on tangible invested capital, plus minor allowance for the intangible items in the balance sheet—goodwill, patents, and so on. (Patents were almost always lumped together with the tangibles in the published "property account.") By a series of formulas I was able to work back from the three known items—taxes reserved or paid, income before tax, and property account—to estimate how much of the property account was in the goodwill category. I incorporated my findings in an article published in *The Magazine of Wall Street*. Barnard Powers, the editor, told me: "Ben, neither I nor anyone else around here can make head or tail of your formulas. It looks as if you've done the whole thing with mirrors. But I've enough confidence in you to publish the article anyway." Given the many possibilities of error arising from misleading published figures, my computation proved later to have been quite accurate. It was only many years later that companies first revealed and then wrote off the water in their capital structures. By that time, however, the asset values had become so unimportant as against the earnings and growth of earnings that these disclosures had no effect upon the financial community.

I might add that my computations reveal that all the 500

million par value of U.S. Steel's common stock, and even a good part of its 360 million of preferred stock, had originally been nothing but water. In a subsequent article, I showed, by similar calculation, that U.S. Steel must have overestimated and overpaid its taxes for the year 1918. This deduction proved to be correct, and U.S. Steel secured a considerable refund from the government.

Although I never made a special effort to secure stock or bond customers for the firm, it was inevitable that a number of connections should develop through the years. Some of these were accounts that I actually managed; they were pretty well restricted to my special field of arbitrage and hedging. The Tassin account continued as one of these. In others, I recall, I assumed no share of losses but received 25 percent of the cumulative net profit. One of these was opened by my old public school chum, Sydney Rogow. My standard procedure was to buy convertible bonds around par and to sell calls against them on the related common stock; or else—in a more elaborate variant—sell the common stock short and sell puts against our short position. The amount received in these puts and calls was substantial and in effect guaranteed us a satisfactory profit on the whole deal, regardless of whether the stock advanced, declined, or stood still. I spare the reader a technical explanation of the complicated business, but it was as successful as it was ingenious.

We had one such elaborate operation going in Pierce Oil bonds in 1919, selling puts against our short position. The market went down; the puts were exercised in part; but a two-hundred share put, worth about $400, was not presented when it expired. It did come in a day late. "Doc" Dougherty from the back office came to me and said the other firm had overlooked the matter and was asking whether the customer would accept it now. I asked Doc what was generally done in cases like that. "Oh," he said, "anyone would be a damn fool who took in a put or call when he didn't have to." Not wishing to be thought a d.f., I said no on behalf of my customer. When I reported this minor windfall to Syd, he suggested that we spend the money by going to Atlantic City together that weekend (with our wives, of course). This we did, staying at the best hotel, spending money with most unaccustomed lavishness, and having a wonderful time. I tell the story to point up an anomaly that has impressed me many times during my life. Businessmen usually have one set of values for their business operations and a much reduced set for their private expenditures. A hundred dollars is a minor matter in a day's business; but at home, it may assume major proportions and cause much dispute between husband and wife. This divergence is natural enough psychologically and is probably necessary to avoid an unsound family budget, but it does give businessmen a sort of dual personality in money matters. In the Atlantic City incident, the special quality and richness of the experience lay precisely in our being able, for this once, to transfer a given sum of money—modest enough—directly from our financial to our private lives.

Uncle Maurice Gerard opened a personal account with me in 1918 which was destined to be crucial for me. It started with a few thousand dollars and proceeded quite satisfactorily. Then, in 1920, he came to me with a startling proposal. He had just finished a job as efficiency expert for General Motors, for which he had received a fee of $20,000. He wanted to add all this money to his account, to retire from his profession, and to live on the profits that I—or perhaps he said "he and I"— would make from his capital. He warned me that since I would now be handling a large fund, I must work on a grander scale than heretofore. I'm sure I did not encourage my uncle in what appeared to me to be a dangerous move, but I accepted the trust. From then on he came regularly to our boardroom and watched the market. He never did any trading himself, nor can I remember his interfering in any way with my conduct of the account. This is extraordinary (if my memory is accurate), for he was by nature a most interfering man.

For the next ten years his decision appeared entirely justi-

fied. Despite monthly withdrawals for living expenses his capital increased to a handsome total. The story after 1929 was
different and most depressing. He died in the thirties, when
the recovery of all our fortunes was just under way. Nonethe-
less he left an estate sufficient to cause major disputes and
hard feelings between his widow and the children of his first
marriage. As arbitrator, I was able to settle the dispute, but
not the hard feelings.

Another client was a schoolmate of mine, Douglas Newman. His account was speculative, and I assumed no advisory
responsibility. It seemed he received his market tips from a
big operator. In due course this operator started to trade
with us, and I witnessed some real speculation. Two stocks
he favored were Mexican Petroleum and Pan American
Petroleum, among the most active and volatile performers on
the 'Change. He traded in good sized blocks, on both sides of
the market. He was always making or losing what seemed
huge sums without turning a hair. He was a born gambler,
with all the attractive features of a gambler's temperament.
He went broke in the decline of 1920 to 1921, and I never saw
him again.

In 1919 we enjoyed a quite typical bull market, marked by
callous manipulation on the part of insiders, and the usual com-
bination of greed, ignorance, and childish enthusiasm on the
part of the public. Some fifteen years later, during my play-
writing period, I decided to write a drama about Wall Street.
The spectacular and tragic events of 1929 to 1932 were then
fresh in mind, but I rejected that period as too extreme to
meet the standards of art. Instead, I went back to my recollec-
tions of 1919 to 1921. I included a number of characters I had
observed in our own boardroom, for example, the monomania-
cal chemist, Riddle, whose only interest was the stock of
American Coal Products, which was going to make him a millionaire, and the Brothers Friedman, shoe store owners, who
had come into our office first to buy the most conservative
bonds available, then to invest cautiously in odd lots of the

"best stocks," and who ended by losing their business and everything else in wild speculations.

Of course, I put myself into the play as hero, the bright young man who profits from someone else's flagrant manipulation without running any financial risks. I conveyed this theme through a plot concerning the transformation of a few small Pittsburgh concerns into a hugely inflated transcontinental oil company. I called the play "Angry Flood"—after the lines from *Julius Caesar:*

> Dar'st thou, Cassius, now
> Leap in with me into this angry flood?

It was never produced, and I do not know where the script is now. It doubtless deserves its oblivion.

Actually, I came through the dangerous period of 1919 to 1921 extremely well. Having learned much from my shattering experience with the Tassin account in 1917, I did not let the angry flood engulf me. My operations were nearly all arbitrage and hedging, affording limited but satisfactory profits, and protecting me against serious loss. A typical operation: one of the speculative favorites of the time was Consolidated Textile, a recent conglomeration of rather second-rate cotton mills. I had bought some of their convertible 7 percent bonds, considering them sufficiently safe, and later, as the common stock advanced, I sold the corresponding amount of shares at prices which assured me a good gain, whatever happened thereafter. Dan Loeb was an enthusiastic bull on the stock and carried many thousands of shares in his customers' accounts. I remember suggesting to him that he replace the stock with the 7 percent bonds, pointing out that he would have virtually the same chance of profit, would run much smaller risks of loss, and would have a better income return into the bargain. To this Dan replied that his customers didn't want to bother with convertible bonds, that they liked to see their stock appearing constantly "on the tape," and that it wasn't necessary to pay the extra point or so for the added safety of the bonds because a big further rise in the stock was absolutely certain. In a year's time the stock had fallen from 70 to 20, while the 7 percent bonds were actually refinanced and paid off at a premium above par.

It's not undue modesty to say that I had become something of a smart cookie in my particular field. Still, I was capable of doing some foolish things in other areas of Wall Street. One day, when I was chatting with Barnard Powers about an article for *The Magazine of Wall Street,* he told me he was thinking of retiring soon, as he had just made a killing in a stock called Ertel Oil. A close friend had invited him in on the ground floor. He had been part of the original group which had bought the shares at $3. A few days later trading had begun on the Curb Market at $10. The syndicate manager had sold out all the participants' stock at this figure, and Powers had just received a large check as his share of the profit. I was unduly impressed by this story and may have uttered some words of envy. Powers good-naturedly offered to let me in on the next deal of this sort, if there was room for my money.

Sure enough, another and apparently promising deal did come along soon afterwards, and a limited participation was available. A new company had been formed, called Savold Tire, which had a patented process for retreading automobile tires. Retreading was then a new idea, and was especially attractive because of the relatively high price of tires. The subscription price of the shares was to be $10, and they were expected to open on the New York Curb at a much higher figure. I think I put up $5,000. As by clockwork or magic, a few days later trading began in the shares at 35, amid considerable excitement. Before the week was out, I had received a check for some $15,000 in return for my $5,000.

In spite of my innate conservatism and commonsense understanding that operations of this kind were essentially phoney, cupidity ruled me. I eagerly sought other deals of this kind, and so did a few friends to whom I had communicated the glad

Ben's father, Isaac Grossbaum, 1896.

Ben's mother, Dora Grossbaum (later, Dorothy Graham) with her three sons — Victor, Leon, and Ben — circa 1896.

Ben at age two, with his older brothers Leon and Victor, circa 1898.

Ben in his twenties, on the Coney Island boardwalk, circa 1916.

Ben and his first wife Hazel, in the mid-1920s.

Ben with his first son Newton and daughters Elaine and Marjorie, Asbury Park, NJ, Summer, 1925.

Ben and wife Hazel, 1934.

Ben standing next to mother Dorothy, shipboard, New York Harbor, 1936. He had come to see his wife and children off on their California vacation.

Ben with daughter Elaine behind him, granddaughter Cathy, and Marjorie, Cathy's mother and Ben's eldest daughter, New York City, 1945.

Ben with son Newton, and holding infant son Benjamin Jr., 1945.

Ben, son Benjamin Jr. ("Buz"), and third wife Estelle, Central Park, New York City, 1947.

Farewell dinner for Ben's son Newton, about to leave for the army, 1953. Left to right, daughter Marjorie, her husband Irving Janis, daughter Winni, daughter Elaine, her husband Daniel Bell, wife Estelle, son Newton, Ben, Walton's wife, nephew Walton Graham, first wife Hazel, her husband Arthur Greenwald, Rose Kraus, Empire Room, Waldorf Astoria, New York City.

Daughter Winni and Ben at Winni's wedding, 1956.

Ben and wife Estelle in Greece, at the Acropolis, 1960.

Ben and Benjamin Jr., Stratford, England, 1960.

Ben and brother Victor with Rev. and Mrs. William Barber at dedication of the Dorothy Graham Memorial Building of the Mount Sinai Baptist Church, Bridgeport, CT, 1965. The Graham brothers donated money for the building as a memorial to their mother.

Ben with son-in-law Irving Janis, daughter Marjorie's husband, in Cezanne's studio, Aix-en-Provence, France, 1969.

Ben at his desk in La Jolla, CA, 1976.

Portrait of Ben in his eighties.

tidings. The price of Savold Tire kept advancing. A large electric sign quickly appeared on Columbus Circle, which first flashed "SAVE," then flashed "OLD," and then deftly combined the two words into "SAVOLD." Soon I heard some exhilarating news. The parent company had decided to license its process to affiliated companies in the various states, and these companies, too, would have shares on the market. Barnard Powers promised to put my money in along with his own.

Action came fast. Four weeks after the original Savold made its appearance, the second company—New York Savold Tire—was organized, and we invested something like $20,000 in the syndicate. Our subscription price was $15 or $20 a share. The stock opened on the Curb at 50, and on sales of 96,000 shares advanced immediately to a high of 60. This was the week of May 10, 1919; I celebrated my twenty-fifth birthday in a blaze of excitement. Promptly I received a fat check for our contribution plus some 150 percent in profits. (No accounting came with the check, and we wouldn't have dreamed of asking for one.) When I announced their share to each of my friends, they all told me to keep their money for them and be sure to put it all in the next deal. After all, there were forty-eight states in the union, weren't there?

Disappointment was in store for us. A third company—Ohio Savold—was duly floated in June, but it was a relatively small affair; we were told that there was no room for our money in that one. It came out on the Curb at 28, advanced the next month to 34, but did not imitate the pyrotechnics of the two previous companies. Nevertheless, we were worried. Was our wonderful party at an end? Powers reassured us. A very large deal was cooking, and we would positively be taken into it. But this company—Pennsylvania Savold—was to be the last of the series. It would have production rights for the whole country except New York and Ohio. Management had decided that more than four Savold companies would be cumbersome and confusing. We neither understood nor approved of this restraint, but we prepared to profit to the hilt from our last gorgeous opportunity. When funds were called for, I sent over some $60,000, half of which was contributed by three wealthy young brothers named Hyman. Maxwell Hyman had been an old schoolmate, friend, and customer. (Once, when we were still bachelors, we had teamed up to win a tennis-doubles tournament at a weekend party at the large summer home of four sisters named Jacobs.)

In August 1919, the world was harassed by a host of problems growing out of the collapse of Germany. But in Wall Street the market continued a headlong advance, especially in stocks of the poorest quality and the rankest speculative flavor. The original Savold was active and strong. In fact, at the beginning of the month it soared to 77¾, but fell back immediately to 53 in the same week. We waited impatiently for Pennsylvania Savold to make its spectacular debut, smacking our lips over our impending killing.

The promised day arrived, but trading didn't begin. There was a "slight delay" for reasons explained neither then nor later. Suddenly all the Savold issues were acting very badly; we wondered what was wrong. Came September and still no trading in our stock. Suddenly a complete debacle occurred in the Savold markets. The parent issue fell to 12½! A few more trades, and then the coup de grâce was announced: "No bid for any of the Savold issues." After October 4 all three companies disappeared completely from the records—as if they had never existed.

I had many conferences with Barnard Powers, who had invested most of his own money, and that of his friends, in Savold. He told me that the arch-promoter who had managed all these flotations had diverted our money to other uses. We could put him in jail, but that wouldn't do us any good. Powers and I formed a committee to represent his victims, and we visited him in his office close to the Curb. I still remember the beautiful blue shirt and expensive cuff links he wore at our meeting. Powers did all the talking, except once. That was when the promoter asked me if I would like to have a very low number for my automobile license. He could get one for me, since he was a close friend of New York Secretary of State Hugo. I declined with cold thanks.

The upshot was that the promoter turned over about 10 percent of our contributions in cash and certificates for shares of companies he had been promoting. In one way or another we managed to sell some of these, and finally returned about 33 cents on the dollar to our respective groups.

What happened to the Savold companies themselves? I never really knew. Presumably they went into bankruptcy—if they ever really existed. There is no trace of any of them in the financial manuals of the following year. All that we—as so-called insiders—ever knew about those enterprises was the (supposed) nature of their business and the number of shares alleged to be outstanding. This information appeared in a flimsy "descriptive circular" of unknown origin. Yet, gullible as we were, we had felt highly privileged to put our money in this manipulative scheme, relying on a speculative public even greedier and more foolish to pay us a huge profit. In the six months between April and September 1919, thousands of shares of the three companies changed hands on the Curb, in trades involving millions of real people's real dollars. But as far as I know, the only thing real about Savold Tire itself was the electric sign at Columbus Square which bore its name. Also, as far as I know, nobody complained to the district attorney's office about the promoter's bare-faced theft of the public's money.

Clearly, Wall Street was quite a different place in 1919 than now. In those days, it reflected the widest imaginable spectrum of ethics. Among themselves, the stock exchange members and the stock exchange houses behaved impeccably. They were highly reliable, also, in the execution of their customers' orders and in their handling of cash and property on deposit. But most of them condoned, and many of them participated in, rank manipulation; they encouraged customers to speculate, knowing full well that nearly all of them would lose heavily in the end. They did virtually nothing to protect the public against gross abuses like the Savold swindle.

Not only many Wall Street brokerage houses but the New York Stock Exchange itself was guilty of these devious practices. It permitted the bucket shops to flourish in their midst with resulting enormous losses to the portion of the public least able to afford it. The bucket shops took a short position which offset their customers' purchases and in one way or another simply pocketed all the margin their customers had put up. To stay within the letter of the law, actual transactions were necessary on both sides of the market, and these trades were made for the bucket shops by certain stock exchange firms allured by heavy commissions. It is impossible that these firms did not know the nature and result of the business they were putting on their books. Nor can I understand how the New York Stock Exchange could have been ignorant of the nature of the bucket shop rackets and the part necessarily played by certain of its members.

Our firm knew pretty well what the bucket shops were up to, and we virtuously refused—on several occasions—to accept lucrative business from them. But I admit that we felt no civic or professional duty beyond such refusal; like all our fellow brokers, we were businessmen, not reformers.

CHAPTER TEN

The Great Bull Market of the 1920s: I Become a Near Millionaire

While I was in school, I held a dozen different part-time jobs in as many fields. But my career in Wall Street included only two: the first was as employee and then junior partner at a brokerage; the second was as head of my own business. Before I went into business for myself, I was seriously tempted to leave the brokerage to become a financial writer for *The Magazine of Wall Street*. Writing had been my early love, and this was an opportunity to combine "literature" with finance. But when I announced my tentative decision to my "partners" at N.H.&L. they managed to dissuade me from it.

After the birth of my eldest daughter, Marjorie Evelyn, in 1920, we decided it was time to try suburban life. We moved to the upper half of a two-story house in Mt. Vernon. It was but a half-block from the Mt. Vernon Country Club, which I soon joined as a tennis member. There we made a number of new friends, joining a rather exclusive clique of Jewish residents of Mt. Vernon, with whom we soon found ourselves associating almost day and night. One couple of this group were the Horvitzes, Aaron and Gertrude. He had been a classmate of Fred Greenman's at Harvard; he had studied law, but never practiced. Instead he became the right-hand man of another classmate, Lou Harris, who with his brothers was operating the highly successful Harris Raincoat Company.

Horvitz got to know a lot about my financial ideas and special methods of operation. The Harrises made a momentous proposition: I was to give up my connection with N.H.&L. to operate a large account for them on a salary and profit-sharing basis. They would put up a quarter of a million dollars and promised that unlimited additional funds would be available if the quality and results of my work should warrant it. I could bring in my other accounts as part of the original capital. I was to receive a salary of $10,000 per year; the capital would be paid at 6 percent and I would then be entitled to one-fifth of any remaining profit—all on a cumulative basis. This proposition was worked out between us in early 1923.

I anticipated some difficulty in getting my firm to let me go. However, luck was on my side. The stock exchange had tightened its rules regarding the amount of free capital required of a member firm in relation to the money it owed as a result of its customers' margin trading. This trading was expanding so rapidly that N.H.&L. could not spare capital for the arbitrage operations I had been conducting with such success. Thus they had reluctantly been forced to say no to some of my good proposals. They could not but recognize that my special talent lay in that field and that it was unfair to ask me to stay in a company where my best activities would be strictly limited. No doubt they calculated also that they would get the benefit of a juicy big account, plus most of the business of my numerous customers, without having to pay the usual tribute to a customers' man. So they released me from my obligations (entirely moral) rather more readily than I had expected. We agreed that I would do all or nearly all my business through them; they in turn would give me the use of an office rent-free, plus a private stock ticker and various other services. (All these concessions were quite permissible then, though later severely limited by NYSE rules.)

The new business was incorporated under the name of Graham Corporation. In order to save part of our corporate income tax, we issued participating bonds to represent all the capital, except for some shares of common stock for voting and other purposes. The old order ended, and the new one began on July 1, 1923, just nine years after I started at N.H.&L. at $12 per week. I made the change without regret. For a long time I had felt that I did not belong in the brokerage business, which repelled me at bottom because I felt (then, at least) that it could prosper only at the expense of its clients' losses.

Not many years ago I read the first volume of the memoirs of Bernard M. Baruch (whom I was to meet in 1927). After recounting the great financial successes which were to make him a millionaire, Baruch recorded a bit of soul-searching. Now that he had achieved fame and a large fortune, what should he do with his life? After paragraphs of discussion, he announced a momentous decision: he would give up the brokerage business, have no contact with or responsibilities to the public, and operate solely for his own account in the stock market. I recall smiling somewhat disdainfully in reading what I considered a lame and egoistical conclusion. How discreditable, I thought, for a highly gifted and enormously wealthy young man to dedicate himself totally to making a lot more money, all for himself. And then, into the bargain, to write this down in his memoirs, without the slightest pang of regret or self-criticism.

But was my decision any more creditable than Baruch's? I too was leaving the brokerage business, where at least I was giving helpful counsel to the public, to limit myself exclusively to a money-making venture. But I was far from a rich man by Wall Street standards. And I had been making good profits for friends and relatives who needed the money. I persuaded the rather unwilling Harris group to allow me to continue to handle my old clients' accounts as part of my corporate capital.

The Graham Corporation operated for two and a half years, to the end of 1925, and was then dissolved. It was a successful venture and returned a high percentage on the capital. I limited investments to my standard arbitrage and hedging operations, plus securities I thought were very cheap on value. The first thing I did was to buy some shares of Du Pont and to sell seven times as many shares of General Motors short against it. At that time, Du Pont common was selling for no more than the value of its holdings of GM, so that the market was really placing no value on its whole chemical business and assets. So Du Pont was greatly undervalued by comparison with the market price of General Motors; in due course a goodly spread appeared in our favor, and I undid the operation at the projected profit.

Another operation ended in a goodly loss with comical overtones. I had come to pride myself on being able to detect both greatly overvalued and significantly undervalued common stocks. I would operate on pairs of such securities, buying a cheap stock and selling a dear stock short against it. One of the stocks I considered overpriced was Shattuck Corporation, the owner of Schrafft's Restaurants. The company was doing well, but the speculators had inflated the price of the shares to what I thought was ridiculous heights. So I bought one of the numerous undervalued issues I was always digging up and shorted a few hundred Shattuck shares against it.

From the start I had arranged a regular weekly luncheon to discuss my exploits. As it happened, these meetings took place at a Schrafft's Restaurant which was a favorite with Lou Harris. When we went short on the stock, we all felt it was against our interest to support the enemy with our lunch checks, so we found another place to eat. Time went by and Shattuck stock continued to go up. (It is an inconvenient characteristic of these popular and therefore overvalued issues that they sometimes continue to be popular and grow more overvalued than ever before they drop to a normal and proper price.) When the price had advanced from our 70 to a most bothersome 100, we held a council of war and decided it was unwise to "fight City Hall" any longer. Anyway, we couldn't expect every operation to turn out well; our overall batting average was high enough; it was good discipline to accept a loss now and then; and so on. So we undid the operation, with a loss of some thousands of dollars. Lou Harris's comment was "Well, one good thing about taking this loss is that I can go back to eating lunch at Schrafft's." We needed the laugh.

But these lunches contributed to the termination of our business relationship. Lou Harris was full of ideas, recommendations, even tips of various kinds picked up at various brokerage houses—very few of which had any place in our carefully worked out scheme of operations. Those that didn't succeed he forgot all about and never mentioned again; those that would have shown a profit he remembered only too well and never failed to bring up at subsequent lunches. After a while I found myself getting fed up with all this second-guessing and Monday morning quarterbacking. It is difficult to work for a long time with a person who has the right to give advice of all kinds without taking any responsibility for what he says.

By 1925 the great bull market was well launched, and more and more people were coming into the market. It was a period in which most customers' men ran discretionary accounts for their clients, which gave them the right to buy and sell what they pleased without specific authorization or orders. Many of these accounts were operated on a fifty-fifty basis, with profits divided evenly between a customer and his customers' man. The customers' man did not have to pay any share of a net loss. I had many friends in Wall Street who told me I was foolish to work for a mere 20 percent of the profits; they could bring me all the money I could handle, with a 50 percent cut (some part of which would be turned over to them).

I began to feel that I was being taken advantage of by the Harrises. At thirty-one I was convinced that I knew it all—or at least that I knew all I needed to know about making money in stocks and bonds—that I had Wall Street by the tail, that my future was as unlimited as my ambitions, that I was destined to enjoy great wealth and all the material pleasures that wealth could buy. I thought of owning a large yacht, a villa at Newport, racehorses—perhaps even mistresses, though I think I was still too naive to include them in my list. I was too young, also, to realize that I had caught a bad case of hubris.

In mid-1925 I proposed a new arrangement to Lou Harris. I would give up my annual salary; instead, after the 6 percent allowed on the capital, I wanted 20 percent of the first 20 percent earned, 30 percent of the next 30 percent earned, and 50 percent of all earned above 50 percent. This seemed to me a neatly logical arrangement. But Lou Harris was horrified at the idea that I would want as much as half of any profit, even after 50 percent had been earned on the capital. We rather quickly agreed to terminate our arrangement and dissolve the corporation at the end of the year. Had the Harrises tried to work out some compromise, I'm sure I'd have agreed, for I have never been stubborn about particular demands. But later I learned that they were already willing to part company with me, even though I had done so well for them. The reason? After two years in intimate contact with my operation, listening to a full explication of the pros and cons of each purchase and sale, they felt that they were now equipped with the brains and expertise to go it alone. Why pay me 20 percent or more of the profits when they might do even better by themselves? So I made my arrangements for 1926, and they made theirs. Since we were both quite satisfied with the change, we parted good friends.

Before writing finis to the Graham Corporation episode, I

must mention an affiliated account bearing the title "Cohen & Graham." The Cohen of the partnership was a thin, myopic lawyer of about 35, also a Harvard classmate and close friend of Harris and Horvitz. He was a student rather than a practicing advocate. He had some capital—$100,000, I think—and Lou Harris was kind enough to make a special arrangement for him, similar to but separate from Graham Corporation. It, too, proved successful, but was terminated at the end of 1925. Why do I mention this unimportant detail? Because the Cohen of Cohen & Graham was none other than Benjamin V. Cohen, destined to join Tommy Corcoran in the famous team of Corcoran and Cohen, the devisers of much important New Deal legislation, and aides to President Roosevelt in pushing laws through a sometimes balky Congress.

Years later, in 1934, Ben Cohen sent me a draft of the proposed Securities Exchange Act—the second of the series of bills that set up the SEC and completely revolutionized many of the practices of the financial world. He asked me for comments. My only observation was about one provision that required that proxy statements sent to stockholders for annual meetings contain, among much other information, "a list of those to whom the statement is being sent." This harmless-sounding phrase meant that a company like AT&T would have to enclose its entire stockholders list of several hundred thousand names. Ben Cohen thanked me for discovering this gaffe and deleted it from the bill, which soon became law.

On January 1, 1926 I transferred my services and my own funds to the "Benjamin Graham Joint Account." Most of the capital was contributed by old friends, including Fred Greenman, Bob Marony, and the Hymans. The financial arrangements were exactly what I had proposed to the Harris group —no salary, but a sliding scale of profit-sharing up to 50 percent. (Little did I think in my egregious self-confidence that six years later I should have to ask, as a favor, that a provision of the original Graham Corporation be revised—to pay me a modest salary in difficult times.) The participants were to receive quarterly payments at the annual rate of 5 percent chargeable against their capital or profits.

The Benjamin Graham Joint Account started with $400,000. Three years later our capital was around 2½ million, most of the addition from profits; a good deal of it belonged to me as the reinvestment of most of my ample compensation plus the earnings on my growing capital. Each year new friends were eager to place funds in the account, the fame of which was spreading by word of mouth. I made no effort to attract additional investments; in fact, I refused to accept money from people whom I did not know personally. But the number of my acquaintances kept growing.

The original group included Douglas Newman, a classmate from Boys High School and Columbia College and a successful lawyer. Some years before he had introduced me to his younger brother, Jerome, who had followed us by three years in the same high school, then had gone through Columbia College and Law School. He had married the daughter of a wealthy cotton converter and mill owner named Reiss. Instead of pursuing the law, he had entered his father-in-law's business and soon was second in command. I had handled some investments for Reiss and also, more modestly, for Jerry Newman.

Towards the end of 1926 Jerry came to see me; he said he wanted to leave the Reiss business and go into mine. Evidently Reiss was not the easiest man to work for. Jerry wanted to come to work for me without salary until he had proved himself of value. He would also make a fair-sized investment, representing the fruits of his work in the cotton business. The idea appealed to me, but I insisted that he accept a modest initial salary of $5,000 per year. This was the beginning of an association which lasted throughout my subsequent business life, ending only with my retirement to California and the dissolution of the two businesses—Graham-Newman Corporation, and Newman & Graham—which had succeeded the Benjamin Graham Joint Account.

Jerry Newman proved invaluable to me almost from the

start. He had a quick intelligence and an excellent head for business in all its practical aspects. He was much better than I at the details of a commercial operation. He was shrewd and effective at negotiating deals of all sorts and was completely honest and dependable—qualities essential for lasting success in Wall Street. However, he was not a theoretician nor especially inventive in the field of finance. I must claim credit for having devised virtually all our strategies and the greater part of our individual transactions. He did have a few negative qualities as well, chief of which was a lack of amiability. He was a hard taskmaster, like the father-in-law whom he couldn't get along with, impatient to have his orders obeyed, critical of small errors, somewhat too tough at a bargain. Yet he was intelligent enough to recognize, in important cases, that the other man must be treated right.

On the whole, Jerry Newman was far from popular, even among his friends, of whom he had many. He had numerous quarrels with close associates, almost always over business affairs. He showed considerable rancor against these opponents, but he surprised me by ultimately making up with almost every one of them. Nearly all have asked me how I found it possible to get along with Jerry Newman for so many years. But in all that time we had virtually no disagreements or arguments. The only one I can remember occurred towards the very end of our partnership: Jerry got the idea that I was unfairly taking all the credit for the success of our business. He was mistaken about certain statements appearing in *Fortune Magazine.*

After two years Newman became an equal partner with me in the management of the business, and he remained so to the end. We had many revenues to divide: salaries, fees for services rendered, profit-sharing arrangements on deals, and so on. We made an agreement, embodied in a very short letter to each other, to divide up all such extraneous or additional earnings on an equal basis. After a number of years, however, Jerry's deals became considerably more important than my outside activities—which were chiefly testifying as an expert in valuation cases. It then appeared proper to both of us to reduce to 25 percent the participation of each in the external earnings of the other.

Again, that certain aloofness in my character—which is one of its chief defects—kept Jerry and me from ever becoming cronies or chums. We were always on the best of terms, but we actually saw little of each other outside business hours. His wife, Estelle, always treated me with affection. I spent a few days at their country house on the New York–Connecticut state line, but I don't remember their ever staying with us. Nor did we ever take a trip together. We spoke very little to each other about our personal lives—including love affairs, a subject which often leads to confidences between male friends far less closely associated than we were.

Jerry lived a far more uniformly successful life, outwardly, than I. He was also much shrewder in handling his personal finances, and he came through the bitter difficulties of the post-1929 years with no real embarrassments. When we started again on our upward path, he was in better financial condition by far; because of that advantage he was ultimately able to amass a much larger fortune than I. But that's not important; more to the point is that on various occasions he was very generous to me. Fortunately for him, unfortunately for me perhaps, I never had the opportunity to be of like assistance to him.

Estelle Newman, of course, had the same given name as my wife. The identical names caused us some amusement through the years, but less confusion than one would have expected, because our social relationship was never really close.

Estelle Reiss was three years older than Jerry Newman and not very attractive. Naturally people said he had married her because of her father's money; but Jerry's kind of ambition made him the last person in the world to want to benefit from anyone's success but his own. Like many women considered homely in their youth, Estelle showed continuous improvement in her appearance as the years passed. She never seemed to look any older, retaining her black hair and her lively glance. Naturally, she took advantage of all that the beautician's art could do to improve upon nature. She had a somewhat distant quality about her, which the well-disposed might have called aristocratic, but the critical—of whom there are always more than needed—described as snobbish or "stuck up." But she was a consummate hostess and always exceedingly gracious to those she liked. Estelle had inherited much of her father's business sense and powers of application. When I became president of the (then) New York Guild for the Jewish Blind, I succeeded in interesting her in our work. She founded the Woman's Division, which did a remarkable job of raising money through a variety of social events. She soon became one of the forces in this increasingly important philanthropy. She and Jerry jointly donated the large funds needed to construct a hospital building on the grounds of our Home for the Blind. It bears their name.

When I reflect on the way lives develop, I am always struck by the large part played by accidental events or circumstances and especially by geographical location. People become close friends because they live close to each other; most love affairs are born out of contiguity, usually aided by the fact that certain *other* parties are *not* on the ground to interfere. Perhaps the chief reason that the Ben Grahams never became social intimates of Jerry and Estelle was that we always lived in different sections of metropolitan New York. For perhaps 25 years the Newmans inhabited a large house in Lawrence, Long Island, an elaborate wedding present from the father of the bride. During all that time I continued to live on Manhattan Island, quite far away. When Jerry and Estelle finally bought an apartment on Fifth Avenue, we had moved up to Scarsdale and had our circle of friends there; then came our emigration to California.

But while distance was to prevent a really close association between the Newmans and the Grahams, propinquity was to establish one between them and my brother Victor. After his marriage in 1927 to the pretty and lively Sylvia Goodman, he bought a nice new house in Lawrence. This made them neighbors of the Newmans, fellow members of the Cedarhurst Golf Club, and soon close friends. Later Victor's reverses forced him to sell their home and leave Lawrence.

Our staff in 1927 consisted only of a stenographer and a bookkeeper. The latter was someone whom I had first met on the tennis courts at the Hunt's Point apartments in the Bronx more than ten years before. We established a close friendship, based entirely on tennis, because he shared none of my other interests. But year after year we played singles, always closely matched, dividing our victories almost equally.

When I played my first tennis match with him, I was an impecunious young man from Kelly Street; his father had a prosperous shoe business, and they lived in one of the best Hunt's Point apartments. A few years later his father died suddenly, and the family's prosperity melted as did ours after my father's passing. He had a modest job with Statler Hotels, and he was glad to come to work for us at a somewhat higher wage.

Each year—except during 1929 to 1933—we paid him a year-end bonus, and in most years we raised his salary. For these purposes he used to prepare elaborate historical exhibits, comparing his earnings with the profits of the business. At our later directors' meetings, the subject of his salary and bonus would come up for discussion every January. He eventually earned as high as $16,000 a year with us, which was really good pay for those days and for the rather mechanical work he did. However, he and his wife lived on a liberal scale (they had no children), and he did some investing of his own with indifferent success. During twenty-five years of association we found him faithful and reliable within the limits of his competence.

He died suddenly in his bed one night of a heart attack. We went over his accounts and discovered some minor peculations, totaling a few thousand dollars. Jerry and I never spoke of this to anyone. Years later I thought of this incident and my reaction to it in reading the *Journals* of the Frères Goncourt. In one entry, they describe the death of their maid, a woman who had served them with unselfish devotion from their childhood. In a second entry they tell their shock at what they had soon discovered about the secret life of this homely and self-effacing domestic, well along in years. She had been spending all her salary to buy the sexual services of various young men. The Goncourts philosophized over the difference between what is seen and what remains unseen in the lives of people quite close to us.

CHAPTER SIXTEEN

The Commodity Reserve Currency Plan

If my name has any chance of being remembered by future generations—assuming that there will be future generations—it will be as inventor of the Commodity Reserve Currency Plan. To describe this plan, I must start with a disclaimer. My formal study of economics was confined to four weeks under Dr. Muzzey at Columbia College in 1912. I quit the course, along with all my others that fall, to take on my daytime job for the U.S. Express Company. When I returned the next February, I could not fit economics into my schedule, and I gave it up with scarcely a second thought. This scanty training in the "dismal science" did not prevent me from setting up later as an authority in the theory and practice of security investment, in corporate finance, and, indeed, in economics, in the professional sense of the term. I have learned whatever I know about economics in the same way I learned about finance—by reading, meditation, and practical experience.

An economic invention of mine has found its way into most of the standard works on monetary theory, and—even as I write this in mid-July 1965—it seems to be in the minds of some economists. The great Lord Keynes wrote an (admittedly ambiguous) article about my idea, and a letter from him to me on the subject will be part of his collected works, when published.

The notion of a commodity-based reserve currency—or CRC, as I shall call it—first came to me in the Depression of 1921 to 1922, when the world had perhaps its first real exposure to poverty in the midst of plenty. There was an excess of production of raw materials generally, as against the effective or cash demand. Commodity prices fell disastrously, producing all kinds of financial embarrassments, which in turn led to increasing unemployment and the vicious cycle of economic depression. From the outset of my study of that depression, with its attendant widespread suffering, I felt that it was all basically unnecessary, and a recurrence should be preventable. If a nation lacks the means of production—in fertile land, manufacturing capacity, technical knowledge—then its standard of living must necessarily be low. But it seems logically absurd for a country like ours, blessed with so many resources, to find itself unable to buy its own products, suffering at once from an excess of goods in the warehouses and too few on the shelves of its families.

Seeking a solution for this anomalous problem, I considered, first, the position of the gold producers. They were exempt from the difficulties that bedeviled the rest of us. No matter how large their output, they could sell it immediately at an assured price—then $20 an ounce. They even gained substantially from the Depression itself since lower wage scales and lower prices for what they needed reduced their production costs and increased their profits. Many economists had suggested plans for stabilizing the general level of prices, but none had won widespread acceptance. The best known at this time was Irving Fisher's proposal for a compensated dollar, under which the amount of gold equivalent to a paper dollar would be increased or decreased to offset a rise or decline in the price level. My own meditation on the problem led me to a quite different solution. A better standard, I felt, was to give a designated bundle or "market basket" of basic raw materials a monetary status equivalent to that which had always been accorded to gold. This meant that owners (producers) of the whole group of commodities in their proper relative proportions could always turn them over to the Treasury for a fixed amount of paper dollars, while holders of paper dollars could always cash them in for the corresponding number of commodity baskets.

For why, I asked, should economic advantages be confined to the gold producers? Were not the ordinary necessities of life as important and as valuable as gold, and were not those who produced them entitled to similar advantages?

In my view, the commodity-reserve proposal had both an active and a passive merit. On the active side, it dealt as directly as possible with the problem of stabilizing the price level by *defining* the dollar in terms of commodities and by establishing a two-way convertibility between the paper dollar and its defined commodity equivalent. In a broad sense this would create a bridge between the world of commodities and the world of money—permitting commodity units to pass over into and be treated as money when they were not needed for consumption, and, conversely, for money to pass back into the world of commodities and consumption whenever necessary. The idea is reminiscent of the famous Biblical story of the seven fat and the seven lean years, and of Joseph's wisdom in storing the surplus against later need.

On the passive side, it did not attempt to stabilize the price of any *single* commodity, as had been tried in the past—quite unsuccessfully—by so-called valorization schemes. My plan permitted each separate commodity to fluctuate in price according to changes in its own supply-demand situation, while maintaining stability (at least within narrow limits) against the bundle of commodities as a whole.

The difficulties of putting this theoretically appealing idea into practice were evidently great. Should dress manufacturers, and countless similar businessmen, be enabled to sell everything they turn out to the U.S. Treasury at a fixed price? Obviously not—there are too many questions about quality, variety, fair prices, perishability, obsolescence, and so on. Most of all, assuming that the government found money to pay for all these things, what would it do with them?

If we pass from the universe of *all* products to the restricted field of basic raw materials, however, many of these problems vanish. A key role in booms and depressions is played by fluctuations in the prices of basic raw materials. As an example, the index of such prices in the United States advanced considerably from 1913 to 1920—as the result of World War I inflation and the postwar boom—but fell precipitously in 1922.

Suppose we limited ourselves to providing an unfailing demand for the most important raw materials? Since these form the basis of the goods economy in general, we could assume that securing their economic position in a way analogous to the assured position of gold would protect both the price level and the effective demand for most commodities against the eroding effects of recurrent depressions. The prices of basic commodities decline far more than do goods generally, and stabilizing the former might well stabilize the prices of consumer products. A comparatively few major raw materials—not more than thirty, say—account for a large part of the value and importance of all primary products. If the price level of these thirty could be stabilized, the economy as a whole might be protected against severe destabilization.

But how to best stabilize the price level of basic commodities? Could we set an unchanging price for a bushel of wheat, another for a pound of copper, another for a pound of coffee, and so on down the line of our thirty products? There are serious objections to doing this. The relative prices of these commodities—each against the others—had always been subject to wide fluctuations, resulting from changes in individual supply-and-demand factors. Are such changes merely temporary? If so, it would be a good thing to suppress them. But they are secular or quasi-permanent, in response chiefly to long-term changes in relative costs of production. A number of efforts had been made in the past to stabilize the price of individual commodities. In 1921 the historical example was sugar, but efforts proved rather unsuccessful. Economists were almost unanimously opposed to the so-called valorization of commodities or services. They liked to refer to the valiant but ultimately unsuccessful attempt to valorize commodities made by the Emperor Diocletian as far back as A.D. 301 as proof that valorization was impractical.

I was conscious of the inherent weakness of any plan to set the individual prices of a number of different commodities. The solution to the problem of stabilization, I felt, lay in fixing, within narrow limits, the price of a bundle or market basket of important commodities *taken as a whole,* while permitting the prices of the several components to vary in accordance with changes in relative supply and demand. In other words, I proposed to give to a properly selected and proportioned group of basic commodities the same monetary status as that then enjoyed by gold. This meant that new money would be issued to producers against, and backed by reserves of, basic commodities.

My meditation about the consumer's situation led me to similar conclusions. The chief cause of depressions in the modern world, I felt, was the public's lack of purchasing power to absorb the increased production resulting from preceding economic booms. I was much impressed by J. A. Hobson's classic work *The Economics of Unemployment,* which theorized about the impact of insufficient purchasing power somewhat as I had. (Hobson's book undoubtedly was an important precursor of the revolutionary thinking of J. M. Keynes.)

This idea came to me during the 1921 to 1922 depression, but I did nothing about it at the time except to discuss it with my Uncle Maurice Gerard, who thought it a good one. I was encouraged also, and surprised as well, to read in *The Sunday New York Times* an article describing a related idea of no less than Thomas Edison, the great inventor. He, too, proposed that new money be created against the deposit of raw materials in warehouses and that the farmers and other producers be compensated with it. But the details of his plan were different and more amateurish than mine: my plan would be simpler to effect and more practical in its consequences. Edison's plan fell into oblivion.

I put the plan aside during the ensuing boom years: I was too busy making money on Wall Street. (These years, by the way, were marked by unusual stability in the price index.)

It was not until ten years later that I published my plan. We were then in the midst of the greatest depression in our history. All the paradoxical malaises of 1921 to 1922 were now being repeated, but to a highly intensified degree. One of the results was an intellectual ferment, marked by the formation of numerous discussion groups, an outpouring of proposed remedies of the greatest variety, and the launching of various movements for bringing about radical changes in the economy. The chief of these was a really radical takeover idea, known as *technocracy*; another was Upton Sinclair's "bootstrap project" in California, known as *EPIC*; a third was the famous Townsend Plan, which advanced the then revolutionary proposal of giving people over sixty a pension of $60 per month.

A group interested in economics was formed and met regularly at the New School for Social Research in lower New York City, under the sponsorship of the school's distinguished president, Dr. Alvin Johnson. I immediately joined the group, which called itself "The Economic Forum." Our purpose was to exchange ideas about how to improve "the sorry scheme of things"—a phrase from *The Rubáiyát* that became our designation for the current economic mess. At one of the sessions in 1932 I presented my plan, in mimeographed form. Actually, I presented four separate plans I had dreamed up. One was the Commodity Reserve Currency Plan, pretty much in its final

form but without the mass of statistics and calculations that
were to be added. A second was an idea for large-scale slum
clearance and its replacement by low-cost housing, with subsi-
dies for the former slum tenants to the extent needed to meet
the new rents. A third was a plan whereby people who had lost
their jobs were entitled to personal credit based on their skills
and experience, credit to be advanced to them by the federal
government in the form of unsecured loans, bearing small or
no interest and repayable on appropriate terms when they
found jobs. While the latter two proposals appeared radical in
the extreme to believers in the laissez-faire philosophy of the
pre-Roosevelt days, they are not far different from schemes
actually adopted in later years.

As a lighter note in my otherwise ponderous memorandum,
I included a fourth proposal suggesting a way that France
could repay the interest and principal on its war debt to us. I
proposed that they do so by annually shipping 40 million bot-
tles of wine, including champagne, and that every American
citizen of voting age receive one such bottle gratis for Christ-
mas. The allocation of wines was to be made by lot, seniority,
or in some other equitable way. It was not a bad idea at all,
introducing both reality and gaiety into the otherwise meta-
physical financial relations of the two countries and at the
same time would dispose of the war-debt question in a practical and pleasing fashion.

Two of the members of our group boldly decided to publish
a magazine which would use our excellent name—*The Economic Forum*—and which would publish as many of the new
proposals as the editors deemed worthy of attention. The
senior editor was a young man named Joseph Mead, whose
later career I know nothing about. The other editor and pub-
lisher was a still younger man, who—although already a member of that stronghold of conservatism, the New York Stock
Exchange—had a keen interest in and an open mind for new
economic ideas. His name was William McChesney Martin.

Little did we suspect that our Bill Martin was destined in a few years' time to be chosen the youngest president of the exchange in history, and thereafter was to become head of the U.S. Federal Reserve System, and thus one of the most powerful financial influences in the world. (I have just read in *Time*, July 2, 1965, that a speech made last month by Bill Martin which referred very briefly to some similarities between the stock markets of 1965 and 1929 led to a paper shrinkage of $34 billion in stock values on the Big Board.)

Editors Mead and Martin asked our forum to submit articles for their magazine. I wrote up my Commodity Reserve Currency Plan under the title "Stabilized Reflation" ("reflation" had then become a popular term to describe a return of conditions from deflation to normal without bringing on the counterevils of inflation). The article was published in the second issue of *The Economic Forum* in 1933. This was the first official presentation to the public of CRC.

In the three decades since I invented it, my brainchild has brought me both gratification and disappointment. One of the psychological high points came at the very start. There was a brief moment of great excitement at the moment of the 1933 inauguration, when I learned that my friend David Podell, the lawyer, had interested his classmate, President-elect Franklin D. Roosevelt, in the idea, and that it was under serious study in Washington as part of the anti-Depression program. Something in the new president's inaugural address led me to think that he favored the commodity-reserve idea; naturally, I was in seventh heaven. I envisaged myself as the famous and honored savior of America's economy and perhaps of the world's. But nothing came of it. However, about two years later, I was visited by an important member of the Department of Agriculture, Louis Bean, a noted statistician and adviser to Secretary of Agriculture Henry Wallace. Roosevelt had formed the Commodity Credit Corporation to support the prices of agricultural products, and it had been buying up large amounts of various farm commodities. Bean saw in my plan a method of financing these commodities by issuing money directly against them, with stimulation to the general price structure by the increase in money in circulation. He gave me considerable personal encouragement about my idea and provided some useful data on prices for the book I ultimately wrote on the subject; but no official action was taken by the Department of Agriculture.

Evidently the CRC was regarded in Washington as too radical an innovation. Certainly it was opposed by Bean's teammate and rival Mordecai Ezekiel, who had other economic nostrums to peddle. So again, nothing happened—and this was to become a familiar sequel over the years. Bean never publicly endorsed the CRC plan, as far as I know; probably it would have been impolitic for him to do so. But he gave me various forms of moral encouragement from time to time and even sent me some historical data which he allowed me to include in my book.

On one occasion Bean had me come to Washington for a meeting with Secretary Henry Wallace. It's funny how certain minuscule details remain in one's memory through the years. As I mounted the main staircase of the imposing Department of Agriculture Building to reach the chief's office, my eye fell on a large mural depicting a varied scene of rural activity and happiness. Beneath it is engraved a Latin saying which begins "Felix si...": "O happy farmer, if you only knew your good fortune." And in the lower right-hand corner the printer had written the source of his verse thus: Virgile, *Géorgiques*. I asked myself in wonderment what these *French* names were doing under a Latin inscription in an American government building? Evidently, a French artist had been commissioned to do the mural, and he hadn't bothered to write "Virgil, *Georgics*," and no one in charge in Washington had even noticed the anomaly. It was as if the building itself had borne on its portals the inscription: *Département de l'Agriculture*.

(A parallel anecdote: the walls of the library of UCLA once bore the familiar words: "Haec studia adulescentiam alunt, senectutem oblectant" ("These studies nourish our youth and comfort our age"). The first time I saw them, I was horrified that Virgil was inscribed as author. To what depths has American culture fallen if a great university doesn't know the difference between Virgil and Cicero? Poor Cicero, who in the very oration in which these words appear, "Pro Archia Poeta," had insisted that all men seek posthumous fame and that even those who wrote tracts entitled "On Despising Glory" took care to add their names as author. Perhaps that vainest of orators rests a bit easier now that "Virgilius" has been erased from the library wall and replaced with his name.)

I don't remember anything of my short conference with Henry Wallace. It must have been quite fruitless; Bean, as a sort of consolation prize, no doubt, gave me the copy of Irving Fisher's *Stable Money* which Fisher had presented to Wallace. The book is still somewhere in my library. Bean later became one of the leading experts in predicting election results and then proceeded to write a book predicting the future movements of the stock market.

In 1936 and 1937 I worked up a book-length presentation of my idea for the CRC. It appeared under the title *Storage and Stability* in 1937. In selecting the title, I had in mind Henry George's alliterative title *Progress and Poverty*. I dreamed that one day *Storage and Stability* would occupy a place in economic literature beside George's masterpiece. I lavished much labor on the book. Facts and references to other writers are supported by a host of notes appearing in the appendix. The book also includes various calculations covering price variations in the proposed commodity unit; these were made by my young niece, who is now Dr. Judith Pool, an authority on hematology. I first asked Macmillan to publish the book, but they politely declined. Though McGraw-Hill had justifiable doubts about the commercial prospects of the book, they agreed to do it—out of deference, no doubt, to the success of *Security Analysis*—but on condition that I guarantee them against loss by taking over unsold copies of the First (2000-run) Edition. This was a far from dignified arrangement, but I acceded to it quickly enough in my eagerness for publication.

How many authors have felt compelled to do the same for works *they* thought would be milestones in the history of thought!

As the book was being completed, another possible entrée to President Roosevelt seemed to arise. Herman Baruch had talked to his brother Bernard about my plan, and it seemed to correspond to some of the great financier's own thoughts. Baruch invited me to his home to talk over my idea. This invitation came just when the galley proofs of *Storage and Stability* had been completed. Our talk went very well. Baruch said he was sure that this was the solution the economy had been waiting for. He would like to associate himself with it, and to present it to President Roosevelt as soon as possible. I agreed to provide him with a set of galley proofs the next afternoon.

I waited as patiently as I could for the result of the Roosevelt-Baruch discussion of the Graham Plan. In a sense I am still waiting, for I have never received any direct information about it. After a week or so my galley proofs were returned to me with a brief and noncommittal note. But Herman Baruch did tell me later, with some embarrassment, that a conversation had taken place, but, apparently, Roosevelt felt that he had introduced so many novelties into the economy that it would be politically unsound to try to pull another rabbit out of the hat. Baruch got the message: there were no practical results or prestige to be gained from my plan so he dropped the matter without a word. I can't help adding: "Just like him."

The hopes I attached to *Storage and Stability* are expressed in a sonnet I composed at the time and entitled "On the First Publication of an Ambitious Work." It begins:

These are the wings that through the nights and years,
Upon the unyielding anvil of my brain,
I forged oblivious...

And it ends with the sestet:

Upon such pinions soared the unlucky one
Who fell lamented in the Icarian sea;
The youth who drove the coursers of the sun
Fell headlong from the upper air—but me
These wings must bear with better luck and higher,
To snatch for man a new Promethean fire.

These comparisons were indeed pretentious; they tempted Fate, and Fate revenged itself in the usual way. I often think of my sonnet when my eyes happen to fall on a copy of Brueghel's sardonic picture "The Fall of Icarus." There, you will recall, a large peasant in the foreground follows his plow, oblivious of anything else, while the son of Daedalus—quite tiny in the distance—is falling helplessly into the water.

A number of academic economists favored my plan, and I was persuaded to launch a publicity campaign to present it to the general public. We needed someone to act as executive director or man-of-all-work for the committee. I found him in an engaging fellow by the name of Norman Lombard. One would have sworn that this was a nom-de-plume, compounded perhaps from Montagu Norman and Lombard Street; but it seems that our man had actually been born with that fascinating moniker. I never knew exactly how he made his living, though I remembered that he was married to a schoolteacher, which no doubt helped a lot. He had been associated with Irving Fisher in the Stable Money Association and later had run some regular monthly economic discussions. We incorporated the Committee for Economic Stability, of which I was chairman. Its name sounds like an imitation of the well-known Committee for Economic Development; not so, because we adopted our name first, just as Pepsi-Cola came before Coca-Cola. We sent out literature and membership blanks, and managed to get fifty or more professors of economics—many with important names—to become members of the committee. But we achieved no results to speak of, despite efforts to make the committee an effective force. I quickly learned that a new economic proposal cannot get financial support from the public unless—like the Townsend Plan for old-age pensions—it promises direct and immediate financial benefits to a specific group, or unless the general emergency is great enough to induce people to approve any idea or slogan that makes vast promises of relief—as was the case with "Technology in the Great Depression." The Committee for Economic Stability has still a sort of legal existence, and even has about a thousand dollars in its bank account, but actually it has been dormant for some twenty years.

Each Sunday for a whole year I looked at the first page of *The New York Times Book Review*, to see if some important economist was hailing *Storage and Stability* as a major solution to the problem of economic depression. After all, the *Times* had done very nicely for me in their review of *Security Analysis*, and this new work was far more important. But apparently the *Times* considered my book just another excursion in the dismal science. They included its name among the new publications—as a matter of form—but did not bother to review it. My disappointment was keen, and only partly lightened by the fact that the book received notices of various lengths in several economic journals, though they were slow in coming.

I was made exceedingly happy when a review appeared in the most important of learned publications, *The American Economic Review*—in the same issue that contained my own article on the subject. It was written by another Graham, Frank D. Graham, professor of economics at Princeton University, and it was favorable, even enthusiastic. Frank Graham was to become an enthusiastic advocate of my idea. His book *Social Goals and Economic Institutions* made a strong plea in favor of a commodity-reserve currency.

Needless to say, Frank Graham and I were not related. However, through contacts following his review, we got to be very close friends, and he became an investor in the Graham-Newman Fund. The similarity of our names produced great confusion in that part of the economic world that took an interest in CRC. Some writers thought we were the same person, others that we were related. Only last month, a professor from Cambridge, a strong advocate of CRC, told me he always thought that Frank Graham and I were brothers. In a footnote to my second book on the subject, I refer gratefully to Frank Graham's support, saying I am glad about a confusion that makes our names almost indistinguishable in this economic sphere. Since Frank Graham had originally been a professor of classics in Canada, I inserted a modified quotation from Horace, which read *Ambos una manet laus*. Horace had actually written, pessimistically, *omnes una manet nox*——"one night awaits (us) all." I changed it to the more hopeful "one praise awaits (us) both" (and added "I hope"). In a gracious note acknowledging my book and its reference to him, Frank Graham wrote modestly "But the 'laus' will go to you alone." His espousal of my scheme and the similarity of our names caused considerable confusion later about which Graham was responsible for the idea.

I recall going down to Princeton at Frank's invitation to take part in a faculty discussion of CRC. In a borrowed academic gown, I dined in hall at the faculty table that evening and listened to a Latin prayer before the meal. I couldn't help contrasting the Victorian atmosphere of the university with that in which modern economists strive to go beyond Adam Smith's economic axioms. That night I slept at Frank's home and made the acquaintance of his gracious wife.

Frank's modest investment in Graham-Newman Corporation was in his wife's name. After his death, his widow let the investment continue. Some years later, she wrote me a charming letter from Europe, telling me how indebted she was to us for her financial independence and her ability to spend the rest of her life as she pleased.

During the years that followed publication of *Storage and Stability*, quite a number of economists, of various degrees of eminence, showed interest in and support of my proposal.

Some of my good friends insisted that a movement should be launched to popularize the CRC idea, in order to bring about its adoption. From the beginning I was convinced that there were only two ways to realize my proposal. The first would be through the advent of another world depression, of the intensity of 1931 to 1932 or even 1921 to 1922, which would force world economic leaders to search openmindedly for a radically new solution to the paradox of want in the midst of potential plenty. The second might be a purely monetary crisis—based, say, on a shortage of international reserves. I could imagine certain financial advisers becoming convinced of the overall soundness of CRC as a means of creating "good money" when it was sorely needed. If ever expert world opinion should become ready for a new and improved formulation of sound money, my idea might be accepted as the best of its kind. On the other hand, I had little confidence in the ability of a propaganda campaign to sell a technical idea like mine to a preponderant segment of the public, nor did I think that mere popular demand—like that for the Townsend Plan—was likely to have much influence on the makers of economic-financial policy.